elevenly: a bitsy assortment.

Christine Cashman

BookLeaf Publishing

elevenly: a bitsy assortment. © 2023
Christine Cashman

Presentation by *BookLeaf Publishing*

Web: www.bookleafpub.com

E-mail: info@bookleafpub.com

ISBN: 9789357440066

First edition 2023

hello. 

ACKNOWLEDGEMENT

הַכָּרַת הַטוֹב.

PREFACE

21 days.
21 poems.

1 sweatshop of stanza.
This book.

hardships + hope.

1

The dichomoty turns complimentary with the
presence of promise.
A dash.
A sprinkle.
A pinch.
A splash.

In a world of turmoil, we all seek serenity and
success.

One small smidgen of optimism offers a
gateway to oasis.

You hold this key.

Seneca said…

Every new beginning comes from some other beginning's end.
Semisonic sang this too.
Initia nova.
Carpe omnia.
There are endless possibilities offered through this thing called life.
Interconnection. Independence.
Reconnection. Separation.
Persistence.
Each future has a past.
Perpetual change is a quality of the ouroboros.
Nothing in the universe can stop you from moving forward or beginning again.

3.

Buy me a bubble tea.
I am yours until this is finished.
Not everything comes so simply.
Dare we feel whimsy?
Dare we feel?
Dare we be?
I am. You are. We.

(untitled).

My inner voice
The truth-teller
The non-sugar coater
Ms. Tell-It-Like-It-Is
Perpetually talking
Endless words feeding this love/hate relationship
Brutal honesty never turning a blind eye
While I intermittently turn a deaf ear
Obstinate old me
You are a big girl now
Momma no longer knows best
Those times forever replaced by this voice
Sanctimonious, acrimonious
My most intimate relationship
My strongest advocate
Me.

human intellect.

inherently imperfect.
inevitability incomplete.
they reason as if it is linear.
this spoon-fed world is not.
fundamental truths guide us.
influential lies divide us.
a mission of mending.
tikkun olam.
repair of the world.

yin. yang. yo.

This is a solar system-generated message.
Kindly do not reply.
Terms and conditions flow from the yin-yang.
Dark, internal, receptive.
Bright, external, exposing.
Fundamental duality of everything in the universe.
Opposite chaotic transmutation.
The sum becomes the whole.

7.

An era exits. An era enters.
Many things remain.
Cycles. Phases.
This landscape of life.
A fresh horizon is born.
Gleaming. Welcoming. Waiting.
I am ready for more.

∞

Erratic.
Adjective.
Having no fixed course.
Wandering through this wonderland of life.
Direction: unknown.
Ever-changing.
Aimless.
Irregular.
Inconsistent.
Eccentric, strange.
Normal. What is normal?
Are we all just a little hop, skip and a deviation
away from being unfulfilled?

…or is this fulfillment?

9.

He could not recall the word in English.
Espontáneo. Spontaneous.
Espontáneo was the wrong word.
Something much darker was essential.
On the other side of dark is light.
The two can be complimentary or contrast.
Two halves have the potential to form the wholeness.
Having gained the power to intelligently face the past,
new dreams actualize with stinging eloquence.
Remaining in the realm of light brings much delight.
One can excite much delight in life's bright, bright light.
Yin and yang is the fundamental duality of all in this universe.
Who is the 'I' that feels like me?
Today I bring my light for all to see.

halfway.

Am I halfway there or halfway to nowhere?
This is a paradox of the human experience.
We are limited beings in an unlimited universe.
Humdrum and vast. Our desires blaze trails.
Our brains (scientifically) shield us from mortal
truth.

Working with the infinite is tricky, tricky
business.

11.

Eleven.
Eleven eleven.
Elevens are a magical message to center.
We experience this guaranteed message twice a
day on our clocks.

Centering can occur on a physical basis and on
an emotional basis: a grounding.
Balance. Balance emotion, thought and spirit.
Balance the masculine and feminine aspects of
our human experience.
Balance work and play.
Balance basics with creativity, dreams,
innovation and goals.

11:11 is where the magic happens.
Balance of life. Balance of love.
We have one minute to welcome this intuitive
and reflective conscious awareness.

11:11 is a confirmation to maintain integrity; to
reaffirm, re-establish and rebalance ourselves.

Balance is a foundation to growth and progress.
We experience this moment in oneness.

☆ 11:11 • make a wish! ☆

Communication. Intuition. Balance.

one. two.

A key to being fully alive — at peace — is
connection; a presence.
Connection can occur on both a physical basis
and an emotional basis.
Feelers feel. Thinkers think. These eyes analyze.
Do you feel me?

The human quality of intellect ushers a
self-awareness.
Cerebral. Visceral.
Mind chattering. Heart churning.
Integration as a goal.
Creatress of my experience.
Let go to connect.
Let's go.

thirteen to unity.

13

Yishuv hada'at is a concept far more profound than 'peace of mind.' A settled awareness.
I settle into a unification with present moment awareness.

The darkness and light hold my thoughts: contrasting and yet supportive. A connection and harmony between the outer level of consciousness and inner self.

The only way to know the essence of something is to fully connect with it. Unity.

resonance.

This abyss of a black, cold, dark night sky slowly
births the beauty of day with each billowing sunrise.

My recent practice is to intentionally and fully make
myself one with this daily cycle.
It is fascinating to see just how much you can learn
from this world by simply increasing your presence
within it.
Vulnerability can be both intimidating and inviting.

"You will never know until you try."
I remember these words of encouragement exiting
my mother's mouth like a skipping record.
In my youth, this concept seemed so dauntingly
vulnerable.

Attempting something new felt like hard work from
the depths of my soul.

New experiences now a cornerstone to my existence
in this enormous world.

Instead of jolting myself awake with light and sound,
I allow the sun's rising rays to support me in this
daily transition to experiential reality.

No artificial light.
No technology.
No noise from humans in a studio.

My morning begins with silence and sounds from my
own backyard. How I enter this doorway to the day
determines the vibrancy of the outcome.

tiny poem.

15

A note from me to you.
Be patient, sweet soul.
Smile.
Life is yours.
This is true.

vitality.

My own mother exited this realm over a decade and a half ago.

Mother Earth has the capacity to still hold us both closely with her in unique capacities.

Opportunities originate when each eyelid opens to allow my visual field a chance to engage with the early morning darkness of this day.

Minute-by-minute, the increasing volume of sunlight nudges my brain…and then radiates to my soul: "Hello sweet sister, I am here to support you for another 9-14 hours."

Someday I will also visit this eternal state of rest. Until then, the saying goes: make hay while the sun shines.

My responsibility is response-ability: I flourish and savor this time in my prime.

LGE.

It looks like we are looking through the looking glass, she said.

We giggled.

That day, we had kaleidoscope eyes.

Decades later, much of the world emanates a different 'looking glass' energy. 'Let normal be the new normal,' their mantra blares.

New normal. New normal.

Alliteration is a powerful rhetorical tool of both poets and totalitarian regimes.

I guarantee my good regardless of their bad.
Bad ideas have an uncanny longevity.
Because of this, we have a greater responsibility to greatness.

For today, reexamine the lens through which you see the world.

Ideas may be bad but humans, as a whole, are inherently incredible.

18.

Try adding a little cinnamon, she said.
A dash of anything can make a often make
dazzling difference.
Input = output.
Infinity, like Heaven, is a concept.
In unending uncovering, this universe is still
abundant in endless mystery.

As a leader, whether through title or influence,
core values affect our outcomes.
We can create quintessential circumstances.

Under the proper conditions, even a dash of dust
has the ability to rise.

Twenty six years ago, a bassline changed my life.

Always. All ways.

Greatness from music of sound waves.
Neurotransmitters know: dopamine function plays
a direct role in music making the brain glow.
When skeptics doubted, the MC still shouted.

Dancefloors crowded.
Decibels flouted.

The tunes now an eternal memory-maker with my
soul deeply shrouded.

I live my advice: If you love it, listen from the core
elements of your existence.

Music stimulates senses across a distinctively
diverse world.

Phenomenon.

bias.
often implicit.
arbitrary, capricious, irrational.
unfair distortion of judgment.
sometimes deliberate and sometimes unintentional.
brains adapted to the savanna environment,
not yet to this intricate modern life.
each person possesses uniquely distinctive
perspectives on values.
many concepts present on individualistic bases.
though complex, we can debias.
useful debiasing techniques exist.
metacognitive strategies empower.
tendentiousness resolves.
equitability.

An an indelible truth is that all good things come to an end.
Fortunately, the bad does too.
Still, what we have ahead is every adventure our psyche
can both imagine and actualize.
In this very moment, what are the best thoughts that you
can think?
I will leave you with this: think these remarkable thoughts.
Think thoroughly. Think unremittingly.
Think widely. Think without limit.
The most effective contributions may have a chance at
experiencing eternal existence.

Thank you.